Thank You Very Much

*The Little Guide to Auditioning
for the Musical Theater*

Thank You Very Much

· · ·

The Little Guide to Auditioning for the Musical Theater

Stuart Ostrow

CAREER DEVELOPMENT SERIES

A Smith and Kraus Book

Published by
Smith and Kraus, Inc.
177 Lyme Road, Hanover, NH 03755
www.SmithKraus.com

First edition: June 2002
Printed in the United States
9 8 7 6 5 4 3 2 1

Cover and Text Design by Freedom Hill Design, Reading, Vermont
Cover photos by Mark Lacy

Library of Congress Cataloging In Publication Information
(Provided by Quality Books, Inc.)
Ostrow, Stuart, 1932–
Thank you very much : the little guide to auditioning for the musical
theater / Stuart Ostrow. —1st ed.
p. cm. — (Career development series)
ISBN 1-57525-301-1
1. Musicals—Auditions. 2. Acting—Auditions. I. Title. II. Series.
MT956.O88 2002   792.6'028
QBI33-352

Preface

The source for this epigrammatic book was a seminar I taught at the University of Houston, called "Auditioning for Theater" wherein I challenged student actors, singers, and dancers to meet the professional standards I used for forty years on Broadway. Although there are mighty tomes written about the agony of auditioning, nothing can compare with the real thing: facing a producer and hearing "Thank you very much," the theater's dreaded euphemism for rejection. Tears and heartache notwithstanding, a few students were inspired, but most of the others dropped out. Better here than in New York. This get-to-the-point guide is an attempt to distill all the printed audition detritus and focus on the central objective: How do you get me to hire you? It is not an actor-friendly-feel-good balm but rather a tough-love approach to survival in showbiz. To paraphrase the great Edmund Kean: Dying on stage is easy, auditioning is hard.

Dedication

To Jamie Rogers, Carmen Alverez, Pia Zadora, Michael Bennett, Baayork Lee, Robert Klein, Edmund Lyndeck, William Duell, Virginia Vestoff, Betty Buckley, Scott Jarvis, Gretchen Cryer, George Hearn, John Cunningham, Reid Shelton, Patrick Hines, Gary Beach, Christopher Chadman, Irene Ryan, Ann Reinking, Northern A. Calloway, Larry Riley, Dorothy Stickney, Dean Pitchford, Priscilla Lopez, Samuel E. Wright, Michael Rupert, Barry Williams, Max Wright, Caroline Kava, Ray Baker, Janet Eilber, Sheryl Lee Ralph, Debbie Shapiro, Tisha Cambell, Jeff Goldblum, Judy Kaye, Timothy Jerome, Robert Downey, Jr., Todd Graff, Anne Marie Bobby, Jane Krakowski, Martha Plimpton, Laura Dean, Alec Mapa, Kathleen Chalfant, Dylan Baker, Michael Cumpsty, John Michael Higgins, and Tom McGowan. See you all at half-hour.

Contents

Introduction

My recurring nightmare is sitting in a darkened Broadway theater auditioning a new show and saying, "Thank you very much" to an actor who has just given a torturous performance of an old song. I see him in my mind's eye take something from his backpack, shout tauntingly: "How dare you say thank you to me!" and then fire a round from his .45-caliber Glock pistol into my head.

Auditioning for a show is the most uncivilized practice for humans since the barbarous exhibition of the Roman gladiators. So why shouldn't today's chorus-line Spartacus seek revenge from a Crassus Broadway producer? A more hopeful outlook would be to think of the audition process as training for The Last Judgment.

There have been many "how to audition" books; the most enlightening ones are by Michael Shurtleff and Gordon Hunt — both of whom were my casting directors. The purpose of this book is to give the professional actor, singer, and dancer a practicing producer's point of view from the other side of the lights. Why did I choose to hire John Lithgow rather than Brian Dennehy or Kevin Spacey to play Gallimard in M. *Butterfly?* Why did Bob Fosse insist dancer Ann Reinking — a nonsinging, inexperienced actress — be Jill Clayburgh's understudy in *Pippin?* Why did Mike Nichols choose Alan Alda, rather than Dustin Hoffman, to play Adam in *The Apple Tree?* My colleagues in the dark — the composer, lyricist, book writer, director, choreographer, and casting director — all have specialized priorities, and our struggle to reach a consensus on who gets the job is the heretofore undisclosed backstage stuff and substance of this esoteric confession.

CHAPTER ONE

Where, When, and How to Get an Audition

. . .

Getting to Know You

There aren't too many MBAs in the theater. Broadway is run like a candy store. Transient producers hire the neighborhood general managers, press agents, casting directors, and sometimes bring their own lawyers and accountants to provide a modicum of credibility to their investors. In other words, everyone employed by the production has an agenda and no one is in charge. It's your opportunity to be the sum of its parts. Check the trade papers or the Internet for information about a new show. Find out the names of all involved and their professional credits. Visit their offices, inquire when auditions are being held, and who is casting, directing (his or her agent?). Research the story, the source material, and especially, the gossip. It will all pay off the moment the stage manager announces your name and you walk into the dark.

THE PRODUCER

Producers outnumber their casts today. They are a consortium, a corporation, or a gathering of landlords. The individual entrepreneur, the lone gun, the stubborn independent is an anachronism on Broadway, so you better do your homework and find out who the CEO of the show's horde is. If you're fortunate, he or she will have had some prior producing experience. Check their credits to ascertain their taste, integrity, and artistic success — albeit an oxymoron these days — and choose your audition material accordingly.

If they are producers that aim for the middle, don't select esoteric songs or scatological dialogue — Irving Berlin and Thornton Wilder will do nicely. If, pray, they are artistic, go for the top: Sing a Sondheim ballad and act the pauses within Pinter. Strong producers in the past, such as David Merrick, Feuer and Martin, and Kermit Bloomgarden, had the final casting say. Be forewarned: Nowadays inexperienced producers defer to their directors — until their show runs into trouble. Then they go nuts and robotically fire the costume designer and replace the second lead.

A further word of caution: Whether you're auditioning for chorus, a principal part, or the lead in a show — and are chosen — *be certain everyone has seen you.* If one of the producers or the dance captain or the composer was absent that day, ask for a second audition so that when the inevitable panic occurs during previews, you're not fired because one of the team never signed off on you. It is essential you audition! I don't care if you're Madonna, Puffy Combs, or Pavarotti; there is no recording, film, or concert presentation that can measure up to reading the text of a new play in person, or having the show's songwriters listen to their work being interpreted by you on stage, wrong notes and all.

I'll never forget John Lithgow calling me from his film location in Montana after reading *M. Butterfly*, beseeching me to be auditioned. It proved a wise decision. My *M.Butterfly* odyssey included a tense moment with the great director, John Dexter, who insisted on the final day of auditions at the St. James Theater that Brian Dennehy play the lead in David Henry Hwang's meditation on men and women, East and West, and appearance and reality.

I thought Kevin Spacey had given the uncommon reading but was too young, that Brian Dennehy was too much of an Irish mug to play a French diplomat, but that John Lithgow had the androgynous look of a sufferer who declares, "I'm a man who loved a woman created by a man . . . to feel the curve of her face, the softness of her cheek, her hair against the back of my hand. . . . I knew all the time somewhere that my happiness was temporary, my love a deception; but my mind kept the knowledge at bay, to make the wait bearable" and should be cast as Gallimard.

Dexter and I walked around the block arguing (he threatened to quit) while the three actors waited for a decision. That's when Dexter let it slip he had had dinner with Dennehy the evening before. My hunch was he had assured the film actor the part was his — before seeing Lithgow's audition — so I told Dexter to go back to the hotel. I informed the actors the majority vote was for Lithgow and that Dexter had quit in protest. It was all a charade. PS: John Lithgow was nominated for the Best Actor Tony Award that year.

THE DIRECTOR

The director is always looking over his shoulder. He is in charge of the show but can be fired by the producer. The mission of directors is to insulate themselves from the vicissitudes of showbiz so they always hire a cast that can deliver their special talent. Bob Fosse hired dancers, Mike Nichols and Jerry Zaks look for comics, and British directors opt for actors with technique.

Do your research, check their credits. Are you going to make them look good? Scratch a director, and you'll usually find a former actor, stand-up comic, or gypsy dancer. Chances are they've experienced the cattle call, bad lighting and acoustics, dumb stage managers, and cement dancing floors; so they want you to succeed.

Don't type yourself out. I've auditioned too many actors who, before they begin, say, "I know I'm not exactly what you're looking for, but—" thereby committing audition *seppuku*. The director has an outline of the show in his head, and he uses the audition process to paint in the details. *All you need to be is a wonderful color.*

During the *Pippin* auditions Bob Fosse chose dancers rather than singers — notwithstanding songwriter Stephen Schwartz's strenuous objections. The climax came when Bobby picked Ann Reinking; a nonsinger and untested actress whose purity of line and extension would have made Pavlova envious. Schwartz drew the line; he would have none of it! Fosse turned to me and said, "Either I get my dancers, or I quit." I sent Stephen home, and Fosse, Reinking, and *Pippin* lived happily ever after. Or at least until Stephen tried to revive *Pippin* without Fosse's direction and dances.

THE CHOREOGRAPHER

Jerry Robbins, Bob Fosse, Gower Champion, Michael Bennett, and Susan Stroman all began their careers as choreographers, so when they counted "five, six, seven, eight," it wasn't only for a dance combination, it was for the days remaining in anticipation of becoming directors. Today — with the exception of the Fosse redux and *Contact* — there are very few dance shows and even fewer original director-choreographers. As long as you are trained in basic jazz, ballet, and/or tap, the choreographer will rank you based on your acting and singing skills. But don't kid yourself, having a good body puts you in the A group.

THE COMPOSER (AS AUTHOR)

Composers, together with the lyricist and book writer (contractually called the *Author*), know there are faults in their work, which they alone detect, and like skilled intuitive builders they can sniff out the dry rot in the beams. Moreover, if necessary, they can dismantle the whole house and begin again. It is vital to win their vote. You'll need it when the audition gets competitive. Composers naturally favor singers based on their musicality, but don't try to show off with something as difficult as "Glitter and Be Gay." "Always" will do.

Since they are collaborating with the rest of the creative team, composers must compromise. Marriage is easy; collaboration is hard. Theater demands it. Egos must be bridled to allow the director, choreographer, lyricist, book writer, designer, or producer — whoever has the best idea at the time — to lead the pursuit for artistic truth.

All you have to be is the best damn singer/dancer/actor in the business. Work on eliminating the break in your voice from chest to head, and practice breath control, intonation, lilt, cadence, accent, modulation, and inflection. And stop smoking. Life upon the wicked stage ain't nothin' like a girl supposes.

THE LYRICIST (AS AUTHOR)

Tell me the story is what the lyricist asks. The other thing they expect is what playwright Tom Stoppard calls "clarity of utterance." Authors find themselves begging individual actors to look after this consonant or that vowel. The word *if* at the beginning of a sentence is a favorite for neglect.

Another cavil lyric writers have is careless pronunciation: i.e., cities (Padua), mythology (Scylla and Charybdis), history (auto-da-fé), foreign words (dites-moi), poet's names (Chaucer), colloquial speech (all 'er nothin') — just to name a few examples of mangled pronunciation I suffered, simply because certain actors didn't take the time to check a dictionary. Consequently I didn't take the time to hire them.

Lyricists are meticulous about accents; so don't throw in a brogue or correct a cockney if it isn't written. "H-A-Double-R-I-G-A-N" is what George M. Cohan wrote, not "dubble," and Alan Jay Lerner's "loverly" is not meant to be "lovely," which is harder to sing. "Berkeley" in "A Nightingale Sang in Berkeley Square" is pronounced "Barkley."

The careful actor will also be rewarded if they research an unfamiliar phrase in order to perform it with confidence. Knowing that "Gazing at you/With the sheep's eye" means to cast or make sheep's eyes of longing and affection, and "And the lickerish tooth" denotes eager, craving, and desirous feelings makes all the difference when you're singing it to the lovesick Salvation Army virgin. Finally, resist your impulse to rewrite a standard. For instance, don't sing "I Get a kick/*You give me a boot*" unless you're Frank Sinatra.

THE BOOK WRITER (AS AUTHOR)

Book writers are the most underrated creators on the team. They dramatize a scene for songwriters to translate into song, leaving the detritus to be integrated as a song cue. Is it any wonder Edward Albee never wrote another musical book after doctoring *Breakfast At Tiffany's?* Since the book for a musical is always in flux (musicals are not written, they're rewritten), it's unlikely you'll be asked to read from the text-in-transition. Do your homework, and bring in a monologue that is in some ingenious way related to the characters. It was better than even money when, auditioning for *Guys And Dolls*, Stubby Kaye and B. S. Pully recited Damon Runyon for Abe Burrows. Acting in a musical is tricky, especially after being off the ground with a song, then returning to naturalistic dialogue. Keeping up the energy is crucial to your reading. George Abbott told his actors, "Fast is good." Frank Loesser hung a rehearsal sign, "Loud is better."

THE SOURCE

More frequently plays, and especially musicals, are adapted from movies, literature, or newspaper stories. In addition, revivals of past theater hits populate Broadway. You don't have to be an archivist to rent the VCR, read the novel or original play, summon up the newspaper article on the web, or buy the original cast album CD to inform yourself about the characters, situation, time, locale, and theme of a forthcoming production. You'll be way ahead of the game when it comes to selecting your audition songs and monologues, and, should you get the part, you'll be better informed than your fellow actors. *Knowledge is the best sanctuary in showbiz.*

THE CASTING DIRECTOR

In addition to Michael Shurtle and Gordon Hunt, some of the other casting directors I worked with were Scott Rudin, Marge Simkin, Howard Feuer, Mike Fenton, Meg Simon and Fran Kumin, Johnson-Liff, Hughes-Moss, and Joanna Merlin. I found the majority to be resourceful, hard working, and caring concerning the actors they recommended. The best ones gave me the feeling they were personally involved in the actor's life, similar to doting parents who proudly detail their progeny's talents and insecurities. The casting director is the most influential voice in the selection of the dramatis personae because they've seen everything the actor has done and can more accurately envisage the range, intensity, and creativity of their stage persona. *Do everything in your power to earn their admiration.*

THE PRESS AGENT

Today's press agent regards the media as a ventriloquist does his dummy, primarily to give voice to his or her producer's premature Pollyannaish casting announcements. If you want the skinny on what new show is in the works before your competition finds out, hang out in a press agent's office. You can get a head start on the type of actor they're seeking and be ready to audition when the star doesn't show.

J. J. Hunsecker, in the film *Sweet Smell of Success,* told press agent Sidney Falco, "You're a cookie full of arsenic, Sidney. I'd hate to take a bite of you." It was memorable Clifford Odets dialogue to punctuate Ernest Lehman's short story-cum-screenplay, but not at all representative of the pussycat press agents who enhanced my career, notably Harvey Sabinson and John and Gary Springer. Unlike Falco, they wouldn't have poisoned you if you visited their offices but more likely would have put your name in a gossip column for the creators to see. The press agent is also a resource to uncover the latest news on who is being considered to direct the play or musical you want. It might be Russell Crowe, and if you have one ounce of imagination, you'll fly to Australia that very night and sing for him in the outback the very same afternoon.

THE GENERAL MANAGER

The GM is the hit man for the limited partnership formed to produce the show. He knows where all the bodies are buried and possesses due bills from theater treasurers, scenic and costume houses, musical contractors, stagehands, trade union representatives, insurance agents, accountants, lawyers, company managers, stage managers, and just about every other department necessary to the running of a production. He is the loyal employee. Street-wise showbiz people know that similar to the company man in *How to Succeed in Business Without Really Trying,* after the greenhorn producers come and go, the general manager will still be there. He's the one who makes sure everyone on the payroll gets paid — general manager first — and he's the one who holds the producer's hand when faced with a difficult decision, and the producer's cojones if he doesn't decide the GM way. He is the Dick Cheney of The Great White Way. The smart GM stays out of the casting game because when the actor is hired, he's the first target on the gripe firing line. Still, it wouldn't hurt to pay homage. A couple of grand will do.

THE INVESTOR

You can find the list of investors in a limited partnership producing a show via the Security and Exchange Commission on the web. Aside from opening night tickets — which they have to pay for — about the only return Broadway angels get today is an actor's gratitude for having arranged an audition. They're your best shot to bypass the protocol and be seen by all. Money talks, especially to the producer, but the talk may not be what you want. The danger is you may be perceived as the investor's bimbo or bimboy and not be taken seriously as an artist.

If you're new in town and the final auditions are in callbacks, OK, use your influence with the investor as a last resort. (Hey, how do you think Marilyn Monroe got started?) However, if you believe in yourself, pay your dues and earn your turn.

In over forty years on Broadway, I've never seen or heard of an undiscovered talent. If you don't get this show, you'll get another. I recall casting *The Apple Tree* when an unknown Dustin Hoffman read for the part of Adam and thrilled us. It wasn't until he tried to sing "Happy Birthday" that our hopes to star him in our musical turned hopeless. Director Mike Nichols' next project, however, was the film *The Graduate* — and he didn't forget Dustin.

THE ASSISTANT

The assistant helps the director organize the details of his or her production and frequently proffers casting suggestions. They are ambitious apprentices who almost certainly have less money than you and work for the exhilaration of discovery by checking out every off-off-Broadway show, village revue, cabaret, and piano bar for new talent. In the fifties, Harold S. Prince was the assistant stage manager for George Abbott, Stephen Sondheim was a gopher for Oscar Hammerstein II, and I plugged songs for Frank Loesser. *Find out who the new assistants are; they are the future.*

THE STAGE MANAGER

The production stage manager has the contradictory task of pleasing both management and labor. He or she is an Actors Equity Association union member and represents the producer's administration backstage. Consequently, he or she pleases neither side. Stage managers too, as with general managers, move from show to show and switch allegiances with the speed of summer lightning. Generally, the stage manager who reads with you has no acting skills — I've never understood why — and will throw your performance into the toilet. Be forewarned and imagine you are acting with Meryl Streep or Robert De Niro. Given the horrific circumstances, it may be the performance of your life. More detail in Chapter Five.

THE ACCOMPANIST

Trouble. The average accompanist is an automaton, pro-grammed to play the identical tempo, style, and melody line for every singer. Is it any wonder auditioning is such a night-mare? The casting director and the stage manager will know who the accompanist will be, and if you can meet the player before your audition, all the better. You must guard against the musician's ennui by carefully preparing your manuscript and talking the accompanist through the arrangement by the piano. *It is crucial to point out the dynamic markings, pauses, and beat out the tempo before you take the stage and sing.* More detail in Chapter Six.

Note: When you audition, you are for sale, and all the above are the buyers. *Don't sell yourself cheap by aiming for the middle. Aspire to the top.* Individually, the team that judges you may be ordinary, but collectively they are a genius. All you have to do is be great.

CHAPTER TWO

How to Dress for an Audition

• • •

The Way You Wear Your Hat

Auditions are not parties; don't show up in your killer dress or Ralph Lauren jacket. The wrong choice of clothing, too much jewelry, a hat, bouffant hair, or any other adornment will distract the auditioner from focusing on your face, body, voice, and character.

BLACK IS BASIC

Bob Fosse had a gimmick; he'd always wear black. When I asked why, he said it matched his disposition. No doubt Bobby's nature was the color of night, but the practical reason was that it accentuated the line of his body when he danced. The shoulder bump, the pelvic thrust, was somehow more sensual in black, and you always knew it was a Fosse rehearsal because all his dancers wore the same absence of color. When an actor arrives in all black to an audition it says to me, "I'm in uniform, paint me any color you see."

COSTUMES AND PROPS

Do not bring your own costume or props to an audition. The job of the designer and the director is to imagine how you look and behave on stage, and you usurp their vision by making your own choices. If, however, the scene calls for you to be sitting, it's perfectly fitting for you to ask if you might have a chair. *Do not bring a chair on stage yourself; ask the stage manager.* Or else pay the stagehands union for a three-hour call.

SHOES

There is no telling what a director will ask you to do at an audition; especially if she or he is interested to see more. *Ladies, wear comfortable shoes.* If you are encumbered with high heels and the scene calls for running to the door to bar your lover from leaving, it will look like something out of *Saturday Night Live.*

CHANGE OF CLOTHING

If it's an audition for a musical, you'll be asked to dance so be prepared to change into your dance clothes. *Gentlemen, no sneakers, bring dance shoes, and ladies, leotards please.* Management is loathe to supply dressing rooms, so underdress as much as you can.

GLASSES?

Unless you wear contacts, if you need glasses to read from a script, bring them to the audition. Sanity rather than vanity.

CHAPTER THREE

What to Bring

• • •

Brother Can You Spare a Dime?

MUSIC MANUSCRIPT

My wife, Ann Gilbert, a former recording artist for RCA Victor, taught music and directed theater and is now vocal coaching privately. She is also the piano accompanist most sought after for professional auditions. Here are the rules for a skilled singer's music manuscript preparation in her own words.

> **Do** give the accompanist clean pages that are punched and in a hardcover three-ring notebook. If you have a long song that has been shortened for audition purposes, cut and paste together exactly what you are singing so the accompanist's eye goes from moment to moment — not frantically trying to find your next highlight marking.

> **Do** highlight each important moment you want the pianist to play: a tag, a play-off, a build, an ad-lib verse, a bell tone,

an intro, a stop, a ritard and, most important, the traditional sixteen bars that many auditions demand. Put these markings in the accompaniment staves, not above the melody line.

Do attach tabs to make turning pages easier, especially on a fast, driving, wordy song, i.e., "Tonight At Eight," "Come Back to Me." *Be specific about instructions.* Most accompanists will play exactly as written unless you indicate your precise needs; a slow 4 tempo, a bright but not too fast tempo, all the highlighted moments, stops, pauses, dynamic markings, etc. Go over the chart briefly, so the accompanist is confident you are a professional, and he or she will escort you accordingly.

Do bring your own transposition — many accompanists do not transpose keys — and with the computer technology available today, you can easily put a song into your desired key.

Do always take your complete audition book of songs. You may be asked to sing several numbers.

Don't give the accompanist six or seven loose sheets of music or a song taped or stapled together horizontally. The upright piano rack can't accommodate the spread, and its short ledge won't hold a homemade arrangement of loose pages.

Don't put your music in plastic sheets. Plastic reflects light, making it harder to read the notes.

BACKPACK

Avoid bringing hiking, camping, parachute knapsacks to the theater. Not only do they clutter the stage — I've seen actors trip over them making their entrance, but they are also dangerous weapons. Neil Simon tells this story. At the *Sweet Charity* dance call after six exhaustive hours Fosse had culled the field down to the final twelve dancers, and, as was his custom, he whispered his thanks to each rejected dancer for coming. One dancer was so shocked that she wasn't chosen, she picked up her backpack and began beating Fosse over the head until the stage manager had to forcibly stop the crazed woman. After it was over, a rather shaken Bob Fosse told the remaining dancers, "No more backpacks on stage, please."

CELL PHONE/PAGER

Turn it off!

TAPE RECORDER

Tape recorders are valuable to bring. If you are winnowed down to sing a song from the score, the composer or musical director will hand you the manuscript music and play and sing the new material once; if you're lucky, twice. You're way ahead of the game if you can record it so that while you're preparing offstage you can refer to the rendition.

FOOD AND WATER

Never eat or drink on stage.

CHAPTER FOUR

What to Sing

• • •

Ac-cent-tchu-ate the Positive

PLAYING TO THE CREATORS

Performers often ask: Do I sing a song written by the auditioning composer or lyricist? Recite an author's monologue from his or her past play? Dance the choreographer's steps from a previous show?

The answer is: Only at your own peril. Creators sing, play, and dance their work in their heads. No actor ever really lives up to what they hear and imagine — that includes the original interpreters of their masterpiece. So why add the burden of their having to judge yet another version, rather than concentrating on you? If by chance you beat the odds and are terrific, the creator, afraid of being accused of showbiz nepotism, may hesitate to vote for you; if you suck, it'll just seem like sucking up.

LENGTH OF SELECTION

Chorus auditions (pink contracts) are differentiated by management's mandatory "sixteen bars only," while for principal parts (white contract), the length of your audition is your decision. The best solution is to prepare two songs. Check with the stage manager, or have your agent ask, how many actors are being auditioned that day. If you are number thirty-three, a short charm song is good; if you are number three, go for the eleven o'clock number. The chorus audition, alas, is a cattle call where every sixteen-bar rendition — usually an up tune — sounds the same. Shake them up and sing the first sixteen bars of a lush ballad.

CHOOSING A SONG

Here are some procedural rules to follow. *Do not render an original song.* The creators are there to judge you. Don't shift their focus by requiring them to judge another songwriter's work. *Do not bring a tape player for accompaniment.* Live actors and musicians perform theater. The director may chat you up on stage before you audition to glean some character insight. *Don't act another character, be yourself.* Finally, when asked what you're going to sing, don't ever announce, "For my first selection" or "And for my second song." Let the auditioners decide if they want to hear anything else.

The following 140 selections, covering nine decades of twentieth-century songwriting, doubtless reflect some accidents of my personal taste; nevertheless the songs, arguably, represent the best in the American musical canon that tell a story, reveal a character, and make you laugh or cry. The stuff of musicals.

THE BALLAD

Here is a list to choose from. Some are offbeat, but most of them are well-known standards; so you must try to endow your rendition with your special insight. There are two kinds of ballads: one can show off your vocal range and texture and, as in the past, volume. With today's theater amplification systems, a sound engineer who has the tessitura of a rap entertainer, alas, controls the singer's volume. So much for the thrill of a crescendo. The other kind of ballad is the one that tells a story. Both are valid, depending on whom you're singing for, but the best of all possible worlds is to be able to combine both thrilling musicianship and dramatic acumen in the same song. Women's selections are indicated with (w), men's with (m).

(w) "Alice Blue Gown" (Joseph McCarthy, Harry Tierney) the popular waltz ballad from the musical comedy *Irene* in 1919 may be thought of today as classical music. Don't be intimidated; it is a lovely authentic curio and will enchant the creators with your ability to evoke the past. Be sure to perform the verse. It is also an especially good choice for lyric sopranos, who struggle with other songs reaching from chest to head tones.

(m) **"All of You"** (Cole Porter), from *Silk Stockings* (1955), had all the sexual overtones necessary to seduce a cold Ninotchka: "I love the looks of you/The lure of you/The sweet of you/The pure of you/The eyes, the arms, the mouth of you/The East, West, North, and the South of you." Given the noticeable absence of heterosexual show songs for men today — including verses — this one can raise the temperature. Don't jazz up the tempo; a languid quality is what is required.

(w) **"Am I Blue?"** (Harry Akst, Grant Clarke) sung by Ethel Waters in the 1929 film *On with the Show,* is a deeply felt torch song that requires an effortless performance. The melody already aches. Just tell the story.

(m, w) **"Anyone Can Whistle"** (Stephen Sondheim) was written for Lee Remick in the 1964 musical of the same title, but it was also — as his caring agent Flora Roberts told me on opening night — "a glimpse into Sondheim's soul." The ballad is a cinch for singers with a limited vocal range, and its uncommon melody engenders a feeling of vulnerability. Sing it gently, once through, no repeats, no remorse.

(m, w) **"April in Paris"** (Vernon Duke, E. Y. Harburg) is a nostalgic ballad that certifies you as a Parisian in love with love. The gorgeous tune is one of Duke's best, and Harburg's Lilliputian lyric of but three unrhymed lines of five, seven, and five syllables, deftly catches thought-flashes of the charm of spring in Paris.

(m, w) **"Autumn in New York"** (Vernon Duke) is yet another stunning melodic remembrance to a fabled city. Throughout the years this ballad has become a jazz standard, but no matter if you sing like Dawn Upshaw or Donald Duck, it casts a spell. Relive it again.

(m, w) **"Back in Your Own Back Yard"** (Dave Dreyer) a tender 1929 reminder — preceding Judy Garland — that there's no place like home.

(w) **"The Ballad of the Sad Young Men"** (Fran Landesman, Tommy Wolf) was included in *The Nervous Set,* a 1959 Broadway anomaly I published solely because I admired this heartbreaking song. Its lyric poetry is matched by a knowing jazz melody, and I managed to persuade Columbia Records to record the cast album, if only to preserve the ballad. Evermore meaningful today in the AIDS plague, I guarantee that the despair will become more telling with each refrain.

(w) **"Baubles, Bangles, and Beads"** (Robert Wright and Chet Forrest, Alexander Borodin) jing-jing-a-lings, a lyrical onomatopoeia from the 1953 Arabian Nights musical *Kismet.* It's a great audition song for women with an iota of iambic, a tittle of trochaic, plus perfect intonation.

(m) **"Better Luck Next Time"** (Irving Berlin) from *Easter Parade,* the notable MGM musical film of 1948, is an affecting ballad from the master — with a bow to the Arlen-Mercer "One for My Baby." Berlin's ongoing melodic line seems inevitable — a joy to sing — and the lack of self-pity in his lyric make you admire the jilted lover evermore.

(w) **"Bewitched"** (Lorenz Hart, Richard Rodgers) from *Pal Joey* has a languid melody and coarse lyrics not for the faint of Hart. The real object of attack is sex, and if you're a rich, ready, ripe little plum, this is your pudding. Think Mrs. Robinson.

(m, w) **"Blame It on My Youth"** (Oscar Levant, Edward Heyman) is a torch song for a naïve lover. A suspiciously Gershwinesque tune sets the tone of the refrain perfectly, but duck the banal verse.

(m, w) **"Blues in the Night"** (Harold Arlen, Johnny Mercer) is a killer song for a big voice. Even though your mama done tol' you, and you're an old hand at being double-crossed, in the end you're left singing the blues in the night. It's a one-act play.

(m, w) **"But Beautiful"** (Johnny Burke, Jimmy Van Heusen) written for Bing Crosby in the 1947 movie *Variety Girl* is one of those seamless ballads that combines rhyme and reason. Van Heusen's melody wears like a good shirt. Even though Crosby croons to women, the feeling is just as viable vice-versa.

(m) **"By Myself"** (Howard Dietz, Arthur Schwartz) is a torch song for a loner; something Hamlet might have considered. The laid-back tune has a hair-trigger bridge (when you think he's going to lose it) then back to calm and resignation. A wonderful character song.

(m) **"Call Me Irresponsible"** (Sammy Cahn, Jimmy Van Heusen) is a love song for a romantic rogue who wins the lady with negative prefixes. Too clever by half, but the lush melody is irresistible.

(m, w) **"Close as Pages in a Book"** (Sigmund Romberg, Dorothy Fields) from *Up in Central Park* (1945) is a memento from the operetta king, blended into a musical theater ballad by America's most brilliant and successful woman lyricist.

(m) **"Corner of the Sky"** (Stephen Schwartz) is the representative "I wish" song from the 70s and will score well with those looking for life's answers. Don't audition it for me.

(w) **"Cry Me a River"** (Arthur Hamilton) is an anguished torch song with the unforgettable enjambment, "Told me you were too plebian/Told me you were through with me and/Now. . . ." A great second selection following an up tune.

(m, w) **"Dancing on the Ceiling"** (Rodgers and Hart) has one of those lyrical verses that makes you love your ceiling more. The musical refrain begins with a simple Rodgers do, re, mi, fa, sol, la walk up the scale, but then you're on your own. Wonderfully imaginative.

(m, w) "Danny Boy" (Frederick E. Weatherly) a sublime Irish folksong (1855) originally entitled "Londonderry Air," composer unknown, has been called the most beautiful tune in the world with good reason. There have been many attempts by lyricists to place the melody, but none more touching than this pastoral eulogy for our Danny Boy.

(m) "Don't Blame Me" (Dorothy Fields, Jimmy McHugh) is another valentine to woo the fair sex, with the ambidextrous Dorothy Fields putting words for a woman in a man's mouth. Jimmy McHugh's music is constantly surprising and although the ballad is sixty-nine years old, it's still a classy standard. A very good choice for a character actor who is seldom thought of as a lover.

(m, w) "Don't Worry 'Bout Me" (Rube Bloom, Ted Koehler) is a gallant love song intended to end a relationship, but we're never sure if the singer really means it. A skillful actor-singer will have a field day interpreting this tortured, schizophrenic declaration.

(m) "Easy to Love" (Cole Porter) isn't so easy to sing but worth the yearning for. Actors with a decent two-octave range should apply. Like so many of Porter's ballads, his music and lyrics make you feel a thought.

(m, w) "Embraceable You" (George and Ira Gershwin) was written as a duet with two refrains, but either gender will benefit by rendering this classic. Ladies, check out, "In your arms I find love so delectable, dear/I'm afraid it isn't quite respectable, dear."

(m) "Everything Happens to Me" (Tom Adair, Matt Dennis) is a wonderful "I get no respect" song with a lush jazz melody. This unique ballad is simultaneously comic and touching, so you must think Charlie Chaplin when you open your mouth to sing.

(m, w) "Ev'ry Time We Say Goodbye" (Cole Porter) is from the half Chekhovian play, half-musical revue, *Seven Lively Arts* (1944). This love song's strange change from major to minor is Porter at his persuasive best. You'd have to be a eunuch to resist.

(w) "Far from the Home I Love" (Jerry Bock, Sheldon Harnick) is an expansive ballad from *Fiddler on the Roof* for a daughter leaving home. Find out how many fathers will be at the audition. They'll be pushovers for this song.

(w) "Faraway Boy" (Frank Loesser) from *Greenwillow* (1960) is a dedicated ingénue ballad for her first love. Charming and full of dreamy references to the one that got away. You'll get points for rediscovering it.

(m, w) "A Fellow Needs a Girl" (Richard Rodgers and Oscar Hammerstein) is a rare ballad for the older performer. Full of wisdom and hope plus a gentle melody, it allows that romance doesn't pass away; it gets passed on.

(m) "A Foggy Day" (George and Ira Gershwin) survives as an unequalled atmospheric ballad from the 1937 movie *Damsel in Distress*. It gives a lonely actor the chance to walk through foggy London town and, with the support of thrilling musical clarity, make the sun and a new love appear. Magic.

(m) **"Fools Rush In"** (Johnny Mercer, Rube Bloom), a precursor to *Come Rain Or Come Shine,* is for the reckless singer with his heart above his head. The melody's equal lack of restraint will melt her heart. Don't croon it.

(w) **"The Gentleman Is a Dope"** (Rodgers and Hammerstein) from *Allegro* is a bittersweet torch song for a lady who thinks she's tough enough to forget that he doesn't belong to her. It will make you a star.

(w) **"Get Out of Town"** (Cole Porter) is a heartbreaking entreaty to your former lover to leave you alone. You are damaged goods and need to convalesce without him: "And when you are near, /Close to me, dear, /We touch too much." But, the lady doth also protest too much — so it's a golden opportunity for you to act the subtext of the song.

(m) **"A Ghost of a Chance"** (Victor Young, Ned Washington) is an opportunity for a leading man to play lack of self-confidence. This broken-hearted ballad will mellow the most bravura singer, and the lyric might even make him look skinny. Be brave; all you have to lose is your cliché.

(m, w) **"Glad to Be Unhappy"** (Rodgers and Hart) was the first song to appropriate cynic-poet Alexander Pope's epigram "Fools rush in (where angels fear to tread)." This ambivalent take on unrequited love is from a wounded lover, painfully using his torch to heal the damage. The verse is as long as the refrain and equally important.

(m) **"Good Thing Going"** (Stephen Sondheim) broods about the possibility of blowing a love affair by taking for granted the good thing he has going. The surprise comes at the end, when we learn the affair is already gone.

(w) **"Guess Who I Saw Today"** (Elisse Boyd, Murray Grand) is a dazzling gem from the revue *New Faces of 1952;* a story ballad with a not-so-fairy-tale ending. Here's a chance for an ingénue to become an adult in thirty-two bars.

(w) **"Hello, Young Lovers"** (Rodgers and Hammerstein) from *The King And I,* had the difficult assignment of convincing audiences a middle-aged widow could feel romance. It succeeded due to an exquisite lyric and a charming melody for a leading lady with a limited vocal range. It'll put wings on your heels.

(m, w) **"Here's That Rainy Day"** (Johnny Burke, Jimmy Van Heusen) is the kind of torch song that elevates the performer to new heights — because the tune is so original — and new lows — because the hurt is so deep.

(m, w) **"How Long Has This Been Going On?"** (George and Ira Gershwin) is about your first kiss. It's a great assignment, especially for the outwardly macho man, or the tough broad, to reveal some wonderment.

(m) **"I Can't Get Started"** (Ira Gershwin, Vernon Duke) could also be classified as a comedy song, but its lament for unrequited love coupled with a lush, romantic melody puts the jazz standard in a class by itself. Check out the three refrains; they got Bob Hope his start in the movies.

(w) **"I Didn't Know What Time It Was"** (Rodgers and Hart) from *Too Many Girls* (1939), is for a former naïve lass who knows what time it is now that she's in love. The ballad's grand bridge will take you off the ground and return you to earth, a lot wiser.

(m, w) **"I Fall in Love Too Easily"** (Jule Styne, Sammy Cahn) is a defenseless ballad for those addicted to love and where playing the game too terribly hard is a losing hand. Poignant and heartbreaking.

(w) **"I Got Lost in His Arms"** (Irving Berlin) is for the singer who has a sound like a room full of cellos. From *Annie Get Your Gun* (1946), it remains an ever-increasing testimony to Irving Berlin's genius for writing effortless melody and thought to make the performing character come into view as romantic and vulnerable. Don't ask me just how it happened; I wish I knew.

(m) **"I Get Along Without You Very Well"** (Hoagy Carmichael, Ned Washington) is a torch song for the chump who was dumped. Of course he can forget her — except when soft rain falls, or when someone's laugh is the same. It will surely break the audition listeners' hearts in two.

(m) "I Talk to the Trees" (Alan Jay Lerner, Frederick Loewe) is a ballad from *Paint Your Wagon* in which Loewe strums Spanish guitars while Lerner has Julio reveal his innermost wishes to a senorita: "I tell you my dreams/And while you're listening to me/I suddenly see them come true." Then a charming beguine coda as Julio imagines an April night, sipping brandy, reading poetry and asking for a dance. Lyric poetry and great musical theater.

(m, w) "I Want to Be With You" (Lee Adams, Charles Strouse) has Adams and Strouse stretching themselves in 1964 with this anomaly from *Golden Boy;* a tender, miscegenetic aria for a black man singing to his intended white bride: "Tonight I'm touching you holding you, world, you're gonna see/We'll make out some how!/Here's my girl and me!/You can't hurt us now!" Thrilling, and impossible because the song is colorblind.

(m) "If There Is Someone Lovelier Than You" (Howard Dietz, Arthur Schwartz) — reportedly Arthur Schwartz's favorite song — is a beautiful serenade with lyrical thoughts to match. For stouthearted men with equivalent voices.

(m) "I'll Buy You a Star" (Arthur Schwartz, Dorothy Fields), from the score to *A Tree Grows in Brooklyn* (1951), never survived, having to compete in the same Broadway season as *Guys and Dolls, The King and I,* and *Call Me Madam.* So here's your chance to play the reformed drunk who promises his wife a star and the moon. What makes this number special is that you want to believe him.

(m, w) "I'm Old-fashioned" (Jerome Kern, Johnny Mercer) was a rare collaboration between these two giants, resulting in this unforgettable ballad Once more, an ascending melodic bridge has you loving and leaping, but landing you safely in an old-fashioned refrain.

(w) "In Buddy's Eyes" (Stephen Sondheim) gives new meaning to ambivalent feelings, with Sondheim's masterful:" So life is ducky and time goes flying/And I'm so lucky I feel like crying" composed for a desperately unhappy housewife trying to console herself in Buddy's eyes. An intense song for a skilled performer.

(m, w) "It Had to Be You" (Gus Kahn, Isham Jones) caused Johnny Mercer to call it the greatest popular song ever written. Once you feel the harmonious rug under the first four bars, you'll understand why it had to be. It is a ballad committed to unconditional love, perhaps unfashionable these days, but I'll bet the audience will yearn to be in your place.

(m) "I'll Be Around" (Alec Wilder) is an arrogant torch song; if that isn't challenge enough for you as an actor-singer, you should go into the insurance business. The tune is accessible so you can create your own emotional dynamics, and the choice to be either hopeful or superior with this dame who has jilted you is a delicate balance.

(w) "It Never Entered My Mind" (Rodgers and Hart) is for the lady in the lurch; a torch song that complains you even have to scratch your back yourself. It's a major ballad for a not so minor heartache and has a great Rodgers tune to chart your way.

(m) "Johanna" (Stephen Sondheim), a love song, not cited often enough as part of Sondheim's oeuvre, is a favorite audition piece for tenors. (I hear it each time I produce a musical and usually hire the actor singing it.) It has uncommon beauty and musical surprise, and although we've been conditioned to 150 years of "Jeanie with the Light Brown Hair," I prefer being sweetly buried in Johanna's yellow tresses.

(w) "Just a Housewife" (Craig Carnelia) gets you audition points for unearthing this 1978 gem. A moving cry for help from one of the legion of pigeonholed women who may have aroused the feminist movement. Do not sing it for conservatives.

(m, w) "Lazy Afternoon" (John Latouche, Jerome Moross), from *The Golden Apple*, enchants us. It has one of those rare lyrics that define the art: "It's a lazy afternoon/And the beetle bugs are zoomin'/And the tulip trees are bloomin'/And there's not another human in view/ . . . And I know a place that's quiet 'cept for daisies running riot/And there's no one passing by it to see." If you sing it, they will come.

(m, w) "Look for the Silver Lining" (Jerome Kern, B. G. DeSylva) reminds us somewhere the sun is shining, and the effortless congregational lift the tune provides will convert even the most jaded pessimist. Gorgeous.

(w) **"Look to the Rainbow"** (Burton Lane, E. Y. Harburg) from *Finian's Rainbow* (1947) is optimistic blarney for a rainy day — passed down from father to daughter — and a chance for you to be a balladeer. This enchanting song is a perfect wedding of music and lyrics, so don't try to improve it with a brogue.

(w) **"Losing My Mind"** (Stephen Sondheim) thinks a lot about the man that got away. The tune wrenches the singer left and right, through sleepless nights, hoping he'll return. What makes this torch song so compelling is the imminent danger she may not recover.

(w) **"Love Me or Leave Me"** (Walter Donaldson, Gus Kahn), despite the jazz versions, should not to be sung up-tempo. It's a torch song by a no-nonsense woman who has got to know, now, whether he wants her to stay or go.

(m) **"Lost in Loveliness"** (Sigmund Romberg, Leo Robin), from *The Girl In Pink Tights* (1954), extols what a thrill she is, what a sight to see, and Romberg doesn't let us down — in this, his last Broadway show — with a stunning melody, surprisingly more musical theater than operetta.

(m, w) **"Make Someone Happy"** (Jule Stein, Comden and Green) is one of those great songs from a flop show. From *Do Re Me* (1960), this effortless piece of advice to make just one heart, one smile, one face, happy may have been the inspiration for that one person, one very special person, in *Funny Girl's* "People."

(m, w) "Mary's a Grand Old Name" (George M. Cohan) can't be topped for honest feeling, especially when you're singing about your mother. There's something there that sounds so square, it's a grand old song.

(w) "Mean to Me"(Fred E. Ahlert, Roy Turk) sings the blues and sighs at the way he treats her, but she's his completely. A hypnotic melody for the powerless lover in you and the men who fanatisize they're the meany.

(w) "Mira" (Bob Merrill) is as technically difficult as it is beautiful. The lyric is equal to the task; first in the verse by establishing repetitive naïve phrases for a sheltered young girl (Lili) eager to join the carnival troupe — "I came on two buses and a train/Can you imagine that? /Can you imagine that?" — followed by a vivid description of the town she's left: "The kind of town where you live in a house till the house falls down." This leads into a wistful refrain, "What I liked the best in Mira is/Everybody knew my name." Lili was hired in a heartbeat, as will you.

(m) More I Cannot Wish You" (Frank Loesser) from *Guys and Dolls*, the show's charm song was given to beloved vaudevillian Pat Rooney Sr., playing fairy godfather to Sarah and wishing her a lover: "With the sheep's eye/And the lickerish tooth." A piece of good fortune for the character actor with a limited voice.

(m) "My Defenses Are Down" (Irving Berlin) — the title sometimes erroneously taken to mean the aftermath of a hurricane (mighty fences are down) — is as rich a ballad as ever written in the American musical canon. If you've got those good baritone low notes, go for it!

(w) **"My Ship"** (Ira Gershwin, Kurt Weill) is an alternating happy and eerie reminiscence of a childhood nursery song. It's an opportunity to be an innocent in a knowing world; waiting for the ship you sing to bring your own true love to you. Not for ingénues.

(m) **"My Time of Day"** (Frank Loesser) is a soliloquy wherein we're given a glimpse into the character's soul; in this case a surprisingly poetic one hidden within a mug's demeanor. Tough intervals (ninths) to sing, but worth the rehearsal.

(w) **"My Yiddishe Momme"** (Lew Pollack, Jack Yellen) was Sophie Tucker's and Belle Baker's signature song to reduce their audiences to tears. The melody is from the God of Abraham and Isaac, but the emotion has no race or accent.

(w) **"Never, Never Land"** (Jule Stein, Comden and Green) was written for *Peter Pan* (1954), and Styne wrote a glorious melody with an octave and five-note range — duck soup for Mary Martin. Be afraid, be very afraid.

(m) **"On a Clear Day You Can See Forever"** (Alan Jay Lerner, Burton Lane) from the 1965 musical of the same title is a towering melody on the Lane that Lerner walks down. So what if you lose your way trying to make sense of the lyric, just act as if you can see forever and evermore.

(m) **"Poor Pierrot"** (Otto Harbach, Jerome Kern) would be Marcel Marceau's theme song, if we could only hear what his pantomime says. The fool in white face loves his fair Pierrette, so how should he know that a girl may vow and forget? An exquisite, tragic song for the clown in you.

(m) **"Real Live Girl"** (Cy Coleman, Carolyn Leigh) from *Little Me* was the one ballad they wrote for comic Sid Caesar. It worked because Sid played it straight, as a shy boy asking for dance. Irresistible; it will fog up their glasses and buckle their knees.

(m) **"She's Funny That Way"** (Richard A. Whiting, Neil Moret) is for the loser who can't explain why he's got a woman, crazy for him. A meaningful bluesy tune underscores his dilemma to end it all and let her go to some better man, but he's only human, coward at best.

(w) **"Somebody, Somewhere"** (Frank Loesser) from *The Most Happy Fella* — the 1956 seminal opera/musical comedy/dramatico-musical work that has endured and promises to be around well into this century — sets the musical's tone with an operatic aria, sung by a musical theater pro. A perfect audition choice for the sung-through musical. (The most memorable performance was Jo Sullivan Loesser singing, and Frank Loesser accompanying: "Somebody lonely wants me to care/Wants me of all people/To notice him there," at our New York apartment the day after she and Frank were married.)

(w) "Someone to Watch Over Me" (George and Ira Gershwin) from *Oh, Kay!* (1926) pensively asks where is the shepherd for this lost lamb? This longing ballad belongs to the ages, and the seemingly effortless melody is a test of musicianship. (Listen to Ann Gilbert's RCA Vik 1956 recording, which obliged Ira Gershwin to write a fan letter.)

(m, w) "Spring Will Be a Little Late This Year" (Frank Loesser) was written for Deanna Durbin in 1943, and it gave Loesser a chance to compose a beautiful melody with difficult intervals, ninths, as he would do again with *My Time of Day*.

(m, w) "The Sweetest Sounds" (Richard Rodgers) from his solo words and music attempt *No Strings* (1962) is the score's best offering. A resonant contralto/tenor melody extols sound, words, sight, and love in thirty-two bars. Someone was watching over Rodgers.

(w) "Teach Me Tonight" (Sammy Cahn, Gene DePaul) can be a sexy ballad for the ingénue if she doesn't exaggerate the double entendre lyric. This is a winning audition song in the right hands and body.

(m) "They Can't Take That Away from Me" (George and Ira Gershwin) changed the way your wore your hat after hearing Fred Astaire sing it in *Shall We Dance*. Don't be intimidated by his relaxed rendition; this great ballad can be sung full out especially from the bridge building to the final refrain: "No, no! /They can't take that away from me!" Thrilling results and no dance steps required.

(**m, w**) **"Till There Was You"** (Meredith Willson) from *The Music Man* is a ballad for the beguiled lover. "There were bells on the hill but I never heard them ringing/There were birds in the sky but I never saw them winging/There was love all around but I never heard it singing." Even the Beatles were entranced. Frank Loesser affectionately called it Meredith's deaf, dumb, and blind song.

(**m**) **"The One I Love (Belongs to Somebody Else)"** (Gus Kahn, Isham Jones) submits that it's tough to be alone on the shelf but worse to fall in love by yourself. It's a wake-up call for the lover trying to dream a happy ending. One chorus confirms it.

(**w**) **"Warm All Over"** (Frank Loesser) swarms all over the emotional landscape, even giving the lady a rush when she touches his hand. A gorgeous, grateful ballad for the waif or wanderer who has found Mr. Right.

(**m, w**) **"What'll I Do?"** (Irving Berlin) as with his "Always," the master songwriter is at his centrifugal best, with questions flying off from the center of a lovesick condition. "What'll I do, when you are far away, and I am blue, what'll I do?" This everlasting song is not for just an hour, not for just a day, not for just a year, but. . . .

(**m, w**) **"Who's Sorry Now?"** (Bert Kalmar, Harry Ruby), written in 1923, is the supreme payback song for a jilted lover. Revenge is never out of date.

(m, w) "You Go to My Head" (Haven Gillespie, J. Fred Coots) is a sip of sparkling Burgundy for the lover intoxicated with romance. A sophisticated ballad that will take all your skills to confirm its sad sobering doubts. This one for your baby gets you sympathy, and the part.

THE UP-TEMPO AND/OR COMEDY SONG

Composers, and chorographers want to be certain you have a sense of rhythm, or, at the very least, can keep a beat. Lyricists and directors want to *see joy, hear the words, and understand the story* you're singing, regardless of the tempo, and if the song contains comedy material, you must enunciate every rhyme. Choose an up-tempo song that has a steady pulse — not one that changes rhythms — and be sure to count off a beat for the accompanist before you begin your audition. This is especially important if you're doing an adlib verse into the chorus.

(m) "Ac-cent-tchu-ate the Positive" (Johnny Mercer, Harold Arlen) was written for Bing Crosby, who Artie Shaw called, "The first hip white person born in the United States." A half-preacher half-hipster song urges you to latch on to the affirmative and not mess with Mister In-between. Have fun with the words and rhythm.

(m, w) "Ain't Misbehavin'"(Thomas "Fats" Waller and Harry Brooks, Andy Razaf) is for lovers who promise to practice self-control when they're separated. In gut tempo and stride-piano style, this ragtime pride and joy comes from the blues, so sing it with soul even though you're thinking of cheating.

(m, w) **"Arthur Murray Taught Me Dancing in a Hurry"** (Johnny Mercer, Victor Schertzinger) is a comic rumba about the risks of taking cut-rate dance lessons. Great for the sad sack or the dippy dame.

(w) **"Beautiful, Beautiful World"** (Jerry Bock, Sheldon Harnick) was the first song Jerry and Sheldon wrote for "The Diary Of Adam and Eve" portion of *The Apple Tree* evening (1966), expressing Eve's original awareness of the beauty around her. It is a diversified, curious, fascinating, bountiful, beautiful, beautiful song.

(m, w) **"Between the Devil and the Deep Blue Sea"** (Harold Arlen, Ted Koehler) is a million-dollar Arlen tune, introduced at the Cotton Club in Harlem (1931) for a show appropriately called *Rhythmania*. The joint is jumpin' — 'cause the bridge swings!

(m, w) **"Button Up Your Overcoat"** (B. G. DeSylva, Lew Brown, Ray Henderson), a playful standard from *Follow Thru* (1928), has a second refrain for the shy man, admonishing his girl to wear flannel underwear when she climbs a tree and not to go out with college boys when she's on a spree. A period show audition song.

(m, w) "**By Strauss**" (George and Ira Gershwin) is a witty waltz for snobbish singers having operetta capabilities and perfect diction. "So I say to ha-cha-ca/Heraus! /Just give me a oom-pah-pah/By Strauss."

(m) "**Come Back to Me**" (Alan Jay Lerner, Burton Lane) demands passion, a lover's impatience, and a singer's breath control. When a doctor loses his susceptible patient in an extrasensory perception episode in *On A Clear Day You Can See Forever* (1965), "Come Back To Me" restores her to reality and Alan Jay Lerner to his former Broadway lyric luster, "Hear my voice where you are! /Take a train; steal a car/Hop a freight; grab a star/Come back to me! / . . . In a Rolls or a van/Wrapped in mink or Saran/Anyway that you can/Come back to me!" Alan, you were great on a clear day.

(w) "**Could I Leave You?**" (Stephen Sondheim) is a sardonic star turn of overdue retribution from a bored wife to her incomplete husband. You must have the chops to finish off this one.

(m) "**Does Your Mother Know You're Out, Cecilia?**" (Dave Dreyer) is a charming, bouncy tune for a guy cautious about robbing the cradle. Try stuttering her name.

(m) "**Don't Put Your Daughter on the Stage, Mrs. Worthington**" (Noel Coward) written in 1935, is the embodiment of British restraint for the first two choruses, until self-control goes out the window at the prospect of this squinty-eyed, bandy-legged, vile, ugly bitch being put on the stage.

(m) "Eve" (Jerry Bock, Sheldon Harnick) was the world's first love song for Adam, about Eve, in *The Apple Tree* (1966). "She keeps filling up the hut with rubbish/Like flowers and plants/And not only is it overcrowded/It's loaded with ants." Bock and Harnick change the mood in the release, from a measured drone to a free-wheeling burst of melody and astonished revelation: "Once I saw her standing on a hilltop/Her head tilted back/The sunlight on her face/Gazing at the flight of a bird/And suddenly I saw that she was/Beautiful/Beautiful, yes, that's the word." An up-tempo, comic epiphany.

(m) "Gimme a Little Kiss (Will Ya, Huh?)" (Roy Turk, Jack Smith, Maceo Pinkard) is yet another old fashioned, proper song for the ardent lover. The tune is buoyant and the sentiment is charming, especially for the character actor with a limited vocal range.

(m, w) "Goody Goody" (Johnny Mercer, Matty Matlock) is a cheeky revenge song to an ex-lover, from the one left singing the blues all night. Now that someone else has broken your heart in little pieces — just as you broke mine — goody, goody!

(m) "Hard-hearted Hannah" (Jack Yellen, Bob Bigelow, Charles Bates, Milton Ager) the vamp of Savanna is the meanest gal in town; via a terrific bump-and-grind tune you can tell the story of her tease 'em and thrill 'em torture and kill 'em methods — even to the point of pouring water on a drowning man!

(m, w) "Heat Wave" (Irving Berlin) from *As Thousands Cheer* (1933) was introduced by Ethel Waters to celebrate that gal who blew in from Martinique and started the heat wave by letting her seat wave. A hot number for men and women recounting her "Can-can," especially if you shake it in a samba tempo.

(w) "He Had Refinement" (Arthur Schwartz, Dorothy Fields) is a rare comic turn for the dopey, trusting dame who longs for the return of her first lover. A comfortable tune and tempo, with hilarious punch lines; from the overlooked *A Tree Grows in Brooklyn* in the copious hit musical 1950–51 Broadway season.

(m, w) "How Ya Gonna Keep 'Em Down on the Farm?" (Sam M. Lewis, Joe Young, Walter Donaldson) is a 1919 vaudeville razzmatazz about the futile expectation of keeping the boys on the farm now that the Great War is over. "Imagine Reuben when he meets his pa/He'll kiss his cheek and holler "oo-la-la!" Sing the verse and strut the chorus.

(m, w) "I Like to Recognize the Tune" (Rodgers and Hart) — although favored by jazz artists, it is a swell audition song for the opinionated champs of melody; those who want to savvy what the band is playing, not what the lyrics are saying. Ironically, this admonition from the preeminent lyric writer of his time.

(m) "If I Only Had a Brain" (Harold Arlen, E. Y. Harburg) won Alan Alda the role of Adam, in *The Apple Tree* (1966) beating out Dustin Hoffman. It's a memorable charm song, for the natural man.

(w) "If I Were a Bell" (Frank Loesser) from *Guys And Dolls* is an exuberant, and a (hiccup) somewhat tipsy, celebration of love. Both stage and screen renditions were ordinary, so here's your chance to, ding, dong, ding, dong, ding!

(w) "If My Friends Could See Me Now" (Dorothy Fields, Cy Coleman) is a playful song about adversity from *Sweet Charity* (1966), when Charity, on one of her tricks winds up in a film star's sumptuous apartment and celebrates her good fortune with a Jimmy Durante strut. This is an especially good audition up-tune for an up-tight legit soprano.

(m) "I'm a Ding Dong Daddy from Dumas" (Phil Baxter) struts into town with an attitude that's irresistible. He's a scamp, and his alliterational song boasts: "I'm a mamma makin' man/And I just made Mary, /She's a big blonde baby from Peanut Prairie." Great fun to play this ding-dong-daddy who could have been the inspiration for Harold Hill.

(m, w) "It's All Right with Me" (Cole Porter). Unrequited love is painful, but leave it to Porter to find something piquant to say about the duplicity of men: " You can't know how happy I am that we met/I'm strangely attracted to you/There's someone I'm trying so hard to forget/Don't you want to forget someone too?" The emotion is universal, and although it would have been scandalous in the *Can-Can* fifties to suggest a woman could have the same ambivalent feelings, imagine you're Madonna today singing, "Their not his lips, but they're such tempting lips/That if some night you're free/Dear it's all right/It's all right with me." Of course.

(m) **"Jeepers Creepers"** (Johnny Mercer, Harry Warren) is as hip an up tune today as it was in 1937. Peepers, weepers, heaters, and cheaters — *Mercerville* — and it's all about her hypnotizing eyes. The perfect audition song to loosen up the classical tenor.

(w) **"Katie Went to Haiti"**) (Cole Porter) is a terrific comedy song about high living and easy virtue in the Islands from the master of double entendre. Good for the "Maude" character in you.

(m, w) **"Life Is Just a Bowl of Cherries"** (Lew Brown, Ray Henderson), another hit song written for Ethel Merman in *George White's Scandals of 1931,* is the perfect outlook for any depression. Its philosophy that we're on a short holiday and should live and laugh at it all will especially resonate with those in a cold, dark theater who have been auditioning actors all day long. Ask the stage manager to put you on last.

(m) **"A Lot of Livin' to Do"** (Adams and Strouse) is a sexy, driving sybaritic celebration from *Bye, Bye, Birdie* (1960) "There are girls just ripe for some kissin'/And I mean to kiss me a few!" Leading men stay away. This is just the song for a nebbish character actor.

(m) "Lulu's Back in Town" (Al Dubin, Harry Warren) conjures up the fabulous lady, and you must see her! A swingin' tune, so shine your shoes, slick your hair, and tell the mailman not to call, 'cause you might not get back home at all.

(w) "Ma, He's Making Eyes at Me" (Con Conrad) is for the skittish ingénue. "Every minute he gets bolder/Now he's leaning on my shoulder/Ma, he's kissing me!" Not for rock stars.

(m) "Miracle of Miracles" (Bock and Harnick) was somehow over-shadowed by the rest of the landmark *Fiddler on the Roof* score — possibly due to its being performed by a comic character — but miraculous nevertheless. It's a song that's written for the passionate voice.

(w) "Murder He Says" (Frank Loesser, Jimmy McHugh) is for an aggravated lover. She's finally found a divine fellow, but his vocabulary is killing their romance. Funny and frantic, especially the second chorus.

(w) "Nobody's Chasing Me" (Cole Porter) was squandered in a misspent *Out of This World* (1950) and is a exceptional example of good-humored unrequited love. A witty, literate up tune, proving even a goddess gets lonely.

(m) "Oh! How I Hate to Get Up in the Morning" (Irving Berlin) copes with a bugler's reveille call by swearing to "get that other pup/The one that wakes the bugler up/And spend the rest of my life in bed." A droll commentary for the sad sack in all of us.

(w) **"Oh, to Be a Movie Star"** (Bock and Harnick) from *The Apple Tree* is a little known comic gem for the waifs and strays in life. Ladies, think Lucille Ball.

(w) **"On the Other Side of the Tracks"** (Cy Coleman, Carolyn Leigh) is an intense, driving, jazz up tune for another impoverished Cinderella, but this one is determined and has an attitude: "Gonna sit and fan on my fat divan/ While the butler buttles the tea."

(m) **"Paddlin' Madelin' Home"** (Harry Woods) is a charming and relentless rhythm song for an equally insistent suitor. Another perfect audition choice to humanize the legit singer.

(m, w) **"Pick Yourself Up"** (Dorothy Fields, Jerome Kern) from the movie *Swing Time* (1936) has an infectious rhythm that makes you want to dance. However, unless you're Fred or Ginger, resist the temptation to tap anything except your vocal technique.

(m, w) **Put On A Happy Face"** (Adams & Strouse) has a terrific enjambment — . . . "mask of tragedy/ . . . you'll be glad ya'de/cided to smile" — and a tune that runs up and down the scale to make any halfway singer sound like a pro. This is a charm song for a charming father figure.

(m) **"Rhode Island Is Famous for You"** (Schwartz and Dietz) from *Inside U.S.A.* (1948) is a punster's dream but with a delightful purpose: comparing her little old Rhode Island rank to the rest of the states. "Pencils /Come from

Pencilvania/Vests from Vest Virginia/And tents from Tentasee/ . . . but Rhode Island is famous for you." Sing all three choruses, and remember it's a love song.

(m) **"Sam, You Made the Pants Too Long"** (Milton Berle) is shtick for the schlimazel who has a lousy tailor. Rarely auditioned, it's a great stage routine for the knowing comic.

(m) **"She Loves Me"** (Bock and Harnick) has the syncopated musical drive of a Count Basie Band, including an eleven-beat "Johnny One Note" build at the end of its bridge to galvanize the last chorus; plus the exuberant lyricism of unguarded feelings. Leading man time.

(w) **"South America, Take It Away"** (Harold Rome) for the daring leading lady who has a sense of humor. From *Call Me Mister* (1946), this aching hostess complains that upon hearing "The rocking of maracas/And the knocking of the knockers/In my carcass!" she'd rather they take all the Latin dances away. A showstopper.

(m) **"Those Were the Good Old Days"** (Adler and Ross) increased the authors of *Damn Yankees* (1955) comedy-character batting average; this time for a slick operator who says he's Applegate, but we know him as the devil. With a languid trombone lick reminiscent of vaudeville, "Ha, ha, ha, ha, /Those were the good old days." Add a tag, paraphrasing Jolson's "Mammy": "I'd walk a million miles or more/For some of the gore/Of those good old days!" and you have another showstopper.

(m) **"Tonight at Eight"** (Bock and Harnick) requires a singer with world-class lungs: "I'll know when this is done if something's ended or begun and if it goes all right, who knows, I might propose tonight at eight." (Inhale.) Worth the effort, it's a winner.

(w) **"The Shape of Things"** (Sheldon Harnick) for *The Littlest Revue* (1956) was an early example of Harnick's wit, erudition and felicity of phrase. The song can be a wonderful surprise, where the conventional lady becomes unconventional.

(m) **"What a Blessing"** (Frank Loesser) "to know there's a devil," is the impish jewel from *Greenwillow* (1960) for the character actor to play a fallen priest. "Oh what blessed relief/That a thief is by nature no thief/And a liar is merely the innocent buyer of lies from the liar in chief." Delightful.

(w) **"A Wonderful Guy"** (Rodgers and Hammerstein) from *South Pacific* (1949) was the emotional precursor to "If I Were a Bell," setting the standard for exuberant outbursts — this one a swirling waltz — "I'm in love, I'm in love, I'm in love, I'm in love, I'm in love with a wonderful guy!" (Five times is the charm.) It's as corny as Kansas in August and a bell ringer.

(w) **"You Can Always Count on Me"** (Cy Coleman, David Zippel) is for the tough, overlooked, yet faithful dame, who keeps coming back for more abuse. Don't sing this for a feminist director.

(m, w) "You Took Advantage of Me" (Rodgers and Hart) is a tricky tune with a blizzard of words, and if done perfectly, will get you points with the songwriters. Rodgers' bridge to the song swings, and will propel you into the last chorus.

(m, w) "You'd Be Surprised" (Irving Berlin) is a sleeper audition song with a big bang for either gender. "He/she doesn't look like much of a lover/But don't judge a book by its cover." It's all in the innuendo.

CHAPTER FIVE

The Dance and Chorus Call

. . .

I Need This Job, I Need This Show

EQUITY AND NONEQUITY

This is what *All That Jazz* and *A Chorus Line* were all about. The real thing is not as glamorous. Actors' Equity Association's catch-22 rule is: You do not qualify as a union member until you get an AEA job, and you can not apply for an AEA job unless you're a union member. So you go to nonequity interviews and chorus calls. They are mandatory but inadequately supervised by assistant casting directors, audition pianists, and dance captains, who seldom have the know-how or daring to suggest an unknown actor, singer, or dancer to their superiors. *You may be the exception.*

LINE AND EXTENSION

In ballet, line is the total effect of the disposition of the dancer's limbs, body, and head in movement or repose.

Extension is the stretching of the leg at an angle from the body. (An extended position can look beautiful with dancers of the jeté type who are loose enough to sustain such a position without straining too noticeably and are therefore said to have a good extension.) If you're a trained dancer, you will score points with the choreographer but only if you are deft in jazz, modern, and tap as well. Unfortunately, the Broadway musical has scant appeal for the genius of Pina Bausch, Mark Morris, William Forsythe, or Mathew Bourne, so beware: Everything is not always beautiful at the ballet on Broadway.

LEARNING THE COMBINATION

The stage will be crowded, so try to have a clear view of the dancer teaching the combination; go up front and dance in the first few rows. *If you hide in the rear, not only will you learn very little, but you will automatically be considered a nondancer.* When you are winnowed down, put into a group of three, and designated to be the point of the trio, you can assume you've aced the combination, so wail. For the others, pray you are put to the left or right of a great point dancer in the triangle, so you can take off his or her steps.

MAKING THE CUT

Of course now you're a star. Once in the A group, you meet friends for drinks at Joe Allen's, live in your own uptown apartment, have an affair with the director, buy Mom a diamond necklace, and put your brother through Harvard. Wrong. This is the most dangerous stage of the process. They usually choose two backups for each actor, singer, and dancer in the event their favorite gets cut, so you've got to be better than you were an hour ago. Stand up, don't run, and count on no one but yourself.

SONG AND READING

Repeat the song you first auditioned, with the original intonations. Chances are you will not be asked to read until after you're hired. That alone should inspire you not to linger too long as a chorus-line gypsy. Go to the principals' audition next time.

CHAPTER SIX

The Cold Reading

• • •

Show Me

BRING SOMETHING TO THE TABLE

The most productive time for the creators to test a new work is during the audition process. They hear their dialogue and songs performed by strangers for the first time and are instantly appalled. Did I write that or does the actor suck? Repetition by widely divergent singers and actors either confirm their worst fears — we have to rewrite — or they delude themselves by hoping the right actor will come along to illuminate their play.

One particular audition, for Archibald MacLeish's play *Scratch*, is etched in my memory. I had flown Douglas Campbell, the distinguished actor and director, to New York to audition for the starring role of Daniel Webster. He read several scenes that left us strangely unsatisfied, and we reluctantly said, "Thank you very much." Campbell sucked in his gut, walked to the stage apron, and reproached us in his best stentorian tones: "You don't know what you're looking for, do you? That's why you have a fail-ure on your doorstep."

Of course we ignored Mr. Campbell and hired a malev-olent Irish actor, Patrick Magee (who was de Sade in *Marat/Sade*) to portray a virtuous American statesman. *Scratch* closed the day after its opening night performance on Broadway, due in great part to our deluded miscasting.

The point is *we are uncertain what we want.* If you've done your due diligence by religiously adhering to Chapter One, you should have some idea of the level of sophistica-tion (or lack of it) regarding the people who might hire you. *Bring something to the table for us to savor.* Use that research to whet our appetites when selecting your song and monologue.

NEW SONGS

What is the lyric story? Given a new song to sight-read cold at an audition, too many singers make a great effort to hit all the notes rather than tell the story. Early voice training, no doubt by middle school music teachers, amateur vocal coaches, classical lieder and operatic instructors, all arro-gantly insisting music is everything when it comes to per-formance is likely to blame, which is why operas come about as close to musical theater as a problem in solid geometry. *Theater is character, crisis, and catharsis.* Study the lyric: Is it meant to be sad, funny, wise, ironic, spiritual? Now put yourself in the song's fiction/romance/anecdote and become the character, the witness, the narrator, or the victim — and *tell the story!*

Learning the tune and tempo. Listen carefully to the composer, musical director, and/or accompanist when he or she demonstrate the song — tape it if you can — and *ask questions*. Can you play the bridge again? How do you pronounce "eleemosynary"? How long should I hold the ending? Do you want a crescendo here? Should it have a jazz feeling? And so on. Bear in mind only the composer and lyricist truly know what's intended — it's too early for the music staff — so try to direct your question to the writers. If they're absent, follow your instinct; you wouldn't have gotten this far without it.

Time to prepare. This is tricky. Cold readings of a song are never conclusive, but first impressions are. Ask for as much time to prepare as possible. You'll want to study the lyric, listen to the tape, get into character, go to the bathroom, call a friend, pray — anything that will buy you time. If you feel time isn't sufficient, ask if you can come back on another day. It's unlikely they'll reschedule, but at least you will have made your point — I'm not ready, I can do better.

The accompanist. It's worth repeating: The accompanist can make you or break you. Listen to the other auditions before you go on. Is he or she playing the wrong changes? Too loudly? Doubling the melody or playing at a sluggish tempo? Or does he or she *swing?* Fill-in when you're out of breath? Play the dynamic markings to punctuate your emotions and smile as if he or she is loving your performance? Forewarned is forearmed.

NEW SCENES

Musical theater auditioners rarely ask for prepared monologues — Shakespeare, Ibsen, Chekhov, or Mamet aren't helpful when choosing second leads for a musical comedy — but they may ask you to read a scene or speech from the new musical's book. The same rules for a new song apply to a new scene as well, along with some additional questions you must ask.

What is the scene about? What is the overall story? Time and place? What has happened before and after the scene? What is my relationship to the other character(s)? Do I have an ulterior motive? Answering these questions will give you important clues to the personality of the character. But you can't get it right on the first reading, especially when you have to read with a stranger.

The stage manager and actor who reads with you. This is yet another torturous ritual in the theater. If the producer has any class, he or she will have hired an experienced actor to read the scene with you. More likely, to save money, it will be the secretary, an assistant casting director, or, worse, the stage manager — any one of them will make you feel you've receded into a high school play. It will take all your cunning and concentration to *act*. I suggest you ask the faux actor to read the lines from offstage, or to turn his or her back to the audience while you're on.

Ask what the writer and director want to see. Asking the right question can reveal your private sensitivities to the buyer-in-chief: "What do you want to see in my character? Am I sympathetic, or unlikable? Am I telling the truth? At what moment in the scene do I change? Do I like myself?

If, however, you are one of those rare, instinctive actors who has a fix on the character, do your thing. In 1988, I offered David Dukes the part of Gallimard, to follow John Lithgow in David Henry Hwang's *M. Butterfly.* Having seen his unforgettable performance opposite Richard Gere in *Bent,* I sensed his affinity to out-of-the-ordinary, dangerous theater but worried he might take umbrage at replacing another actor. Wrong. Not only did he accept eagerly, but also wasn't concerned that John Dexter, our illustrious director, was unavailable and that I would direct his first appearance in the play.

It became obvious during rehearsals why David was so secure. He had a clear vision of how the character was to be interpreted — quite different than Lithgow's yet equally candid — and never once paid attention to anything I said. Thank God. His debut brought the *New York Times* critic back to the O'Neill Theater, where he revised his original review, joining the majority to help us win the Tony Award for Best Play.

CHAPTER SEVEN

Auditioning with Others

. . .

Together Wherever We Go

LISTENING TO EACH OTHER

"And so, over the years . . . we settled into our routine, Butterfly and I," the duped diplomat said. "She would always have prepared a light snack and then, ever so delicately, and only if I agreed, she would start to pleasure me." He then confessed, "But mostly we would talk. About my life. Perhaps there is nothing more rare than to find a woman who passionately listens." John Lithgow's *M. Butterfly* monologue ran approximately three minutes, but our eyes shifted between him and B. D. Wong, who was *listening* so intently, the tragedy was palpable. *The point is you must not just wait for your cue to speak or sing, but act when you are silent.*

ARE WE DOING THE SAME SHOW?

Although it is not always possible, try to spend a few minutes with the actor reading with you to make certain you both can bring the scene to fruition. Agree on its objective. Is it funny, sad, whimsical, heartbreaking, sexy? You may know the drill, but your collaborator may not.

CHAPTER EIGHT

The Callback

• • •

It's Not Where You Start (It's Where You Finish)

DRESS

Another title for this chapter could be "the road gets rougher, lonelier, and tougher." You're closer to being hired but the competition is stiffer. Try to make your appearance exactly the same as your last audition for these folks, including your hairstyle and perfume. If you didn't shave the day of your audition, repeat the stubble. They have probably seen 100 actors in the last few days. Since you're being called back, *make them remember you*.

MATERIAL

To paraphrase Ira Gershwin again, your great beginning will have seen the final inning should you fail to repeat the song you first auditioned. They want to be reassured their early take on you was as good as they imagined it. Don't get cocky and try on a different personality. Then again, this is showbiz, and there are those rare exceptions.

Chris Chadman, an amazing gypsy — and later a choreographer — when auditioning for *Chicago* following his years in *Pippin,* didn't want to repeat being Lewis, Pippin's conceited, androgynous half-brother. He decided, therefore, to audition as a sexy rock idol, singing "A Lot of Livin' to Do" from *Bye, Bye, Birdie* and surprised Bob Fosse by his versatility and masculinity.

He not only was awarded the part of Fred Casely, the cocksman that Roxie shoots when he walks out on her, but was given the master of ceremonies opening speech, setting the hard-hitting tone of the musical: "Welcome. Ladies and Gentlemen, you are about to see a story of murder, greed, corruption, violence, exploitation, adultery, and treachery — all those things we all hold near and dear to our hearts." His performance prompted me a few years later to hire Chris as Jeff Goldblum's understudy in *The Moony Shapiro Songbook*. Moral? There are no rules. If you have the passion, sell the action.

SECOND SONG

Assuming your first audition song was a ballad, most likely they will ask for an up tune for the second song, and vice versa. Be prepared. I would suggest you have two new songs for each category, and ask them to pick a preferred one. This will get you points. ("If she's this resourceful in an audition, imagine her inventiveness for my show!")

SPACE TO YOURSELF

While you are waiting to go on, find a private place back-stage or in the bathroom and tell the stage manager where you'll be. This is the moment you need to be by yourself — to summon up the blood and get into character. Also, resist being Ms./Mr. Congeniality by comparing notes with the other actors. They'll steal your ideas in a heartbeat: "Everything about it is appealing. . . . "

THE PROPOSITION

I went into the theater to meet women. The irony is I became a producer and realized I could never command the show if I started fooling around with the cast. Sure, others are going to hit on you. Tell them what the street kids say to drug dealers: "Talk to the back, 'cause the front don't want to hear it." If that doesn't work, ask them if they want to get married.

CHAPTER NINE

Replacing an Actor

• • •

I'll String Along with You

DURING THE COMMERCIAL RUN

Too often the director and choreographer are off doing another show, so it falls to the authors, stage manager, and producer to audition replacements. They usually choose a singer/dancer/actor who is an imitation of the person who originated the part. Why? It's less work and cheaper to put a duplicate into the show — which is one reason why long runs lose their luster. Alas, dear actor, in addition to scrutinizing the replacement's performance, you should also check with the wardrobe mistress to find out if you fit the costume. Wear a rip-off of it to the audition, copy the character's hairstyle, walk, and accent, and be an angel — sing the song in the same key. (They will not pay for an orchestral transposition.) Undoubtedly, you'll want to bring something personal to your interpretation of the original song, dance, or scene. Don't. Wait until you get the part. You may not be an angel, but until the day that one comes along, they'll string along with you.

PREOPENING

Before a show is frozen, however, anything goes. For example, we had trouble casting a ladylike Martha Jefferson for *1776*, (we had mistakenly hired a comedienne and then had to fire her), so when unknown Betty Buckley, looking like a cheerleader and straight off the plane from Texas, began her audition by saying "Howdy!," I thought we had hit bottom. "You're very pretty, Miss Buckley, but not the type, thank you very much," I said. "Won't y'all least hear me sing?" replied a future Norma Desmond, and before I could say no, she was into "Johnny One Note," and wiped us out. After her thrilling performance I turned to Peter Stone and Sherman Edwards and asked, "If you were Thomas Jefferson and hadn't seen your wife for six months, wouldn't you finish writing the Declaration of Independence the minute Betty Buckley walked in the door?" That is exactly how Peter rewrote the scene.

Afterword

Auditioning as Metaphor

We all have to audition, in one way or another, for our way of life. I was a twenty-one-year-old buck sergeant in the United States Air Force in 1953: producer/director of various camp shows and weekly network radio broadcasts during our Korean police action. The Air Force wanted a morale-building national stage show along the lines of Irving Berlin's *This Is the Army* and Moss Hart's *Winged Victory* to commemorate the fiftieth anniversary of powered flight, and they asked me to produce it.

I convinced the colonel in charge that professional writers were needed (Frank Loesser in particular) and hitched a C-54 ride to Mitchell AFB in Long Island. I gave the elevator man at Manhattan's Warwick Hotel twenty bucks to tell me what floor Mr. Loesser was on and rang the doorbell in the tower suite.

It was a gamble that changed my life. Looking like a small dapper Anthony Quinn and as warm and funny and smart as anyone I have ever known, Frank Loesser invited me in and we drank up the night. He had the gift of bringing out the best in you, and I never sounded better to myself. *Although I didn't realize it at the time, I was giving one hell of an audition!* We exchanged loop-to-loop concepts for the Air Force musical, and I swear he even wrote a lyric for a general who gambled: "Old crap-shooters never die, they just stay faded," he ad-libbed at the piano. After a couple of deals before dawn, Frank announced he would write the score only if I hired Abe Burrows to write the book. Was I dreaming? I had lunch the next day with Burrows at the 21 Club and was back in Washington, D.C. that afternoon with an agreement from two Broadway giants — the creators of *Guys and Dolls* to write the USAF *Conquest of the Air.* The colonel thought I was a genius and gave me a three-day pass.

Surprisingly, the following week I was told to appear before the Senate Government Operations Committee's Permanent Subcommittee on Investigations. I was asked what my political affiliations were, was I ever a member of the Labor Party, wasn't my father born in Kiev, Russia? It was frightening. What did this have to do with putting on a show for the Air Force?

It wasn't until my colonel vouched for me and explained that McCarthyism was in the air — synonymous with political opportunism and public character assassination — and that Abe Burrows was under investigation for alleged Communist sympathy that I realized what Loesser's intention was. If the United States Air Force would hire Burrows, the witch hunt would stop. It was why Frank agreed to write the musical, giving up a year of his life and putting his reputation on the line. It was called friendship. In the end my chicken colonel wouldn't fight the barnyard cocks, and I had to tell Frank Loesser and Abe Burrows the Air Force couldn't use them.

"You're a born producer, kid," Frank said, "and when you get out of the service, you've got a job." Sure enough, Loesser's Frank Music Corporation hired me, and I worked my way up the ladder from song plugger, to press agent, to governor general of the Hollywood office, to vice president and general professional manager at twenty-eight. It was seven years good luck, and I like to think there was enough of J. Pierrepoint Finch in me to have earned Frank's farewell letter when I quit to produce my first solo Broadway musical. It arrived with a $10,000 check, a lot of money in 1961 — the year, *How to Succeed in Business Without Really Trying* opened — which simply, but to me grandiloquently, said, "I believe in you. Love, Frank."

The point is: *Creative people take chances.* I took a chance by flying to New York and giving the hotel elevator operator my last twenty bucks. Loesser took a chance and hired me. The chimney sweep Ella, in the *Passionella* Part III of *The Apple Tree,* beseeches us, "I'm not asking much. It's not as if I want to be a *rich,* beautiful, glamorous movie star. Or even a *well-liked* beautiful, glamorous movie star. I just want to be a beautiful, glamorous movie star for its own sake." At least that's honest.

Too many of you, reading this, are kidding yourselves. It's a grueling profession and precious few actors ever reach the top. So why are you on this journey? If you can answer the question without using the words *money, glamour, fame, romance,* or *sex,* you have the right to be taken seriously. I don't wish to hurt your feelings, but neither do I want to pussyfoot. To that end, I suggest you either stop reading here (I'm not kidding — it's something I often do when I realize that the writer, albeit always a stranger and not a friend or colleague, is about to tell me something useless and destructive) or pour yourself a stiff one and read on.

If you are prepared for "Thank you very much" on a daily basis, continuous study and training without an immediate reward, taking two or three minimum wage jobs to pay the rent (or asking your parents to support you), having no HMO, dental plan, Armani suits, or hairdresser appointments, only fast food for breakfast, lunch, and dinner, and going to bed at 9 PM — you might have a chance. *If, however, no one pays you for singing, acting, or dancing within three years, find another life.*

STUART OSTROW was Frank Loesser's apprentice and became the Vice President and General Manager of Frank Music Corp., and Frank Productions, Inc., the Broadway coproducers of: *The Most Happy Fella, The Music Man, Greenwillow,* and *How to Succeed in Business Without Really Trying.*

As a solo producer, his many original award-winning Broadway and West End productions include: *M. Butterfly,* which won the Tony Award for Best Play, *Pippin,* and *1776,* which received both the New York and London Drama Critics Awards as well as the Tony Award for Best Musical. He also produced *The Apple Tree,* produced and directed *Here's Love,* was the associate director of *Chicago,* and the author of *Stages* on Broadway.

Mr. Ostrow established the Stuart Ostrow Foundation's Musical Theatre Lab in 1973; a nonprofit, professional workshop for original musical theater — the first of its kind. Since its inception, the MTLab has presented thirty-two experimental new works, including *The Robber Bridegroom* by Alfred Uhry and Robert Waldman, *Really Rosie* by Maurice Sendak and Carole King, *Up From Paradise* by Arthur Miller and Stanley Silverman, and *Medea* by Robert Wilson.

Stuart Ostrow is a trained musician, choral conductor-arranger, and clarinetist. He has served on the Board of Governors of The League of New York Theatres, the Advisory Committee of The New York Public Library, and the Board of Directors of the American National Theatre and Academy. He has also served on The Overseer's Committee to visit Harvard's Loeb Drama Center, and was a founding panel member of the Opera-Musical Theatre Program of the National Endowment for the Arts.

He produced the original Broadway production of *La Bête,* which also won the Olivier Award for Best Comedy, and he was honored as Producer of the Year by the National Alliance for Musical Theatre. He is the Distinguished University Professor of Theatre at the University of Houston and the author of *A Producer's Broadway Journey.* Mr. Ostrow recently served as a member of the Pulitzer Prize Drama Jury and is the Chairman of the Board of Trustees for the Institute for Advanced Study in Musical Theatre.